Our **Wild**™
World
SERIES

Turtles

NorthWord Press
Chanhassen, Minnesota

DEDICATION
For Jody, Glenda, Hope and Gina
—D.D.

© NorthWord Press, 2003

Photography © 2003: Brian Kenney: cover, pp. 25, 28, 36, 38-39, 41; Allen Blake Sheldon: pp. 4, 6, 12-13, 19; Mako Hirose/Seapics.com: p. 5; Michael H. Francis: pp. 9, 18, 22; Mark Newman/Tom Stack & Associates: p. 10; Ed Reschke: p. 14; James E. Gerholdt: pp. 16-17; Wayne Lynch: pp. 26-27; Kitchin & Hurst/Tom Stack & Associates: p. 31; Doug Perrine/Seapics.com: back cover, pp. 21, 32-33, 34, 37, 44.

Illustrations by Jennifer Owings Dewey
Designed by Russell S. Kuepper
Edited by Judy Gitenstein
Cover image: Eastern box turtle (*Terrapene carolina*)

NorthWord Press
18705 Lake Drive East
Chanhassen, MN 55317
1-800-328-3895
www.northwordpress.com

Library of Congress Cataloging-in-Publication Data

Dennard, Deborah.
    Turtles / Deborah Dennard ; illustrations by Jennifer Owings Dewey.
        p. cm – (Our wild world series)
    Includes index.
    Summary: Discusses the physical characteristics, behavior, habitat, and life cycle of turtles.
    ISBN 1-55971-862-5 (hardcover) – ISBN 1-55971-861-7 (softcover)
        1. Turtles—Juvenile literature. [1. Turtles.]. I. Dewey, Jennifer, ill. II. Title. III. Series.

QL666.C5D443 2003
597.92--dc21

                                                        2002043127

Printed in Malaysia

10 9 8 7 6 5 4 3 2 1

Our **WILD**™
WORLD
SERIES

Turtles

Deborah Dennard
Illustrations by Jennifer Owings Dewey

NorthWord Press
Chanhassen, Minnesota

TURTLES ARE fascinating animals that may be found in deserts, swamps, rain forests, rivers, streams, lakes, and even yards. Turtles are 1 of the 5 kinds of reptiles. Turtles are related to other reptiles, such as snakes, lizards, crocodiles, and alligators. They all belong to a group scientists call *Class Reptilia*.

Turtles are ancient animals that are like the other reptiles because of their scales and their cold-blooded bodies. That means their body temperature is the same as the air or water around them. Turtles are different from other reptiles because they have bony shells. Other reptiles do not.

A turtle's shell grows from its backbone. A turtle cannot climb out of its shell or live without its shell. As the turtle grows, its shell grows. A turtle cannot trade its shell for another one.

Turtles can pull their heads inside their hard shells for safety.

Green sea turtles use their flipperlike feet to swim great distances through the ocean.

Turtles, such as this Mississippi diamondback terrapin, like to sun themselves on a log over water. At any sign of danger they fall into the water—and safety.

There are 3 words used for animals that are turtles: turtle, tortoise (TOR-tiss), and terrapin (TERR-uh-pin). The name "turtle" is often given to turtles that spend most of their time in water. The name "tortoise" is often given to turtles that spend most of their time on land. The name "terrapin" is often given to water turtles that are eaten by people.

These names can be used in different ways and are sometimes confusing. Not all turtles live the way their name suggests. Some tortoises like to go swimming and even find animals and plants to eat in the water. Some turtles spend most of their time on land.

In this book, when talking about these animals in general, the word "turtle" will be used. Any reptile with a shell, no matter how it looks or how it lives, will be called a turtle. The words tortoise or terrapin will only be used when describing a certain type, or species (SPEE-sees), of tortoise or terrapin.

No one is sure where the word "turtle" comes from. It may have come from the Spanish word *tortuges,* (tour-TOO-gess). Spanish explorers used this word to describe turtles and turtle eggs that were an important food eaten by sailors on long journeys. The word "tortoise" may have come from the French word *tortisse* (tor-TESE). *Tortisse* is a word that describes a turtle's bent and crooked legs.

Scientists call all turtles *Chelonians* (kih-LOW-nee-unz). There are about 225 species of turtles in the world.

Turtles
FUNFACT:

All diamondback terrapin males have a dark stripe across the mouth that looks like a mustache.

Map turtle

Spiny turtle

Chilean tortoise

Soft-shelled turtle

Different types of turtles have different types of shells. Some are soft and leathery. Some are rounded. Some are ridged, and some are even spiky for protection.

Turtles can be found in most places in the world, from deserts to rain forests to oceans. They can live anywhere that the weather does not stay below freezing most of the time. They have shells that are made of 2 parts: upper and lower. The upper shell is called a carapace (KAIR-uh-pace). The lower shell is called a plastron (PLAS-tron). If you look at the inside of a carapace you can see the backbone and the way in which the rest of the shell grows from it.

The 2 shell parts are joined by supports that are like bridges. These are on both sides of the body and between the front legs and back legs. The shell is covered in bony plates and in layers of large, thick scales called skutes (SKOOTS). Turtle shells grow by becoming thicker and wider. If the turtle is injured (IN-jurd), or hurt, the shell can bleed.

To make the shell extra strong, the bony plates grow together in a zigzag pattern. Not all turtle shells are alike. Some turtles have hinged shells that close up like a box. Some turtles have soft, but tough, leatherlike shells.

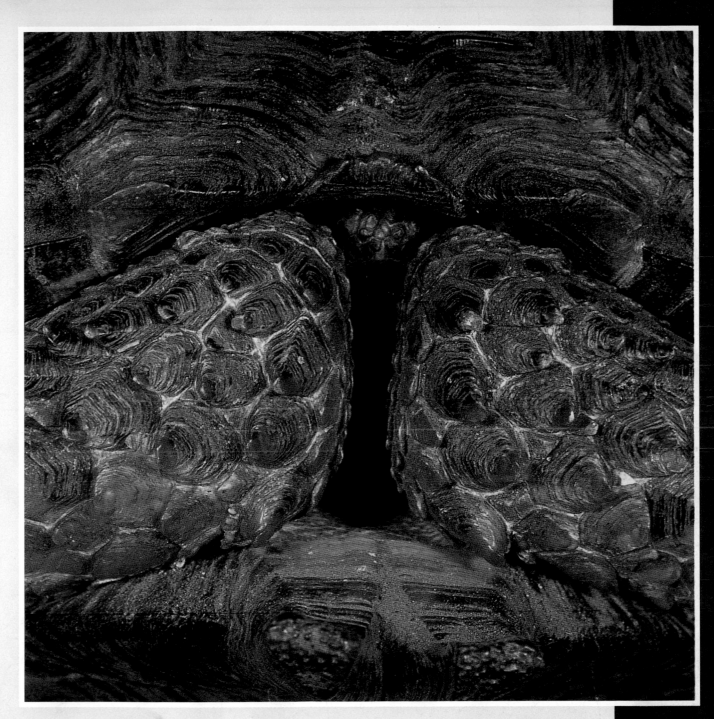

This Texas tortoise can protect all of its vital organs inside of its shell. Here only the front feet are showing.

9

This giant tortoise eats the pads of a prickly pear cactus but spits out the spines of the plant.

All turtles use their sharp, horny jawbones to bite and pull food apart. Some turtles use their front feet to hold onto food as they eat. This makes it easier to tear the tough leaves and shoots. Some turtles hunt the animals they eat. Others just wait for a meal to come wandering by.

Different turtles have different diets. Turtles that live on land usually eat plants. Some land turtles eat both plants and meat. Other turtles are mostly carnivores (KAR-nuh-vorz), or meat eaters. Some species have very special diets, such as the map turtle. This North American turtle has lines on its shell that look like roads on a map. It eats almost nothing but snails.

Turtles may eat different foods at different times of the year. During spring and summer many turtles may eat insects, worms, and other small animals. When the weather gets cooler and insects and worms are hard to find, they may switch to plants and berries. Turtles may not eat much food during the winter, or they may hibernate, or sleep through the winter without any food at all.

Many young turtles start life as meat eaters, especially while they are still growing. Often they switch to a plant diet as they grow older and need fewer calories (KAL-or-eez) and less protein. Turtles can go for a long time without eating at all, if they have eaten enough earlier to store fat in their bodies.

Young turtles need a lot of calcium (KAL-see-um) to strengthen their growing shells. Calcium is a mineral found in some plants and soils. To get enough calcium, many turtles eat sand or chalky soil. Some turtles also swallow small rocks or stones to help grind up the food in their stomachs.

Turtles
FUNFACT:

Turtles do not have teeth. Instead they have hard, bony jaw ridges that they use for eating.

Water is important to many kinds of turtles, but some tortoise species need very little water. The plants they eat give them the water they need. Other turtles wait until the rains come and water is easy to find. Then they drink a lot of water. The desert tortoise, a species from the American Southwest, can drink as much as 40 percent of its body weight in water in just 1 hour. All too soon the water from the desert rain will be gone.

Turtles
FUNFACT:

Sea turtles drink salt water then squeeze out the extra salt through special tear glands.

The desert tortoise drinks water that collects after a rain, or it may dig into the sand with its strong front feet in search of water underground.

Turtles that eat plants seem attracted to the colors yellow and red, such as the red of the strawberry being eaten by this box turtle.

Animals explore the world around them using the senses of sight, hearing, taste, touch, and smell. The senses of sight, hearing, and smell are most important to turtles. Like snakes and lizards, turtles have an organ in the roof of their mouth that allows them to both taste and smell the air as they breathe it in. This organ is called a Jacobson's organ (JAY-cub-sunz OR-gen). It is named for the person who discovered its use.

The sense of smell helps male and female turtles find each other during mating season. Turtles can even smell underwater.

The sense of sight is important to turtles. Scientists have learned that turtles see in color. They use their color vision to help find food. They seem to like food that is either red or yellow. Sea turtles can see very well underwater. From underwater they even can see up onto land. Since sea turtles leave the water when it is time to lay eggs, this helps them to find their way. To protect their eyes from salt, wind, and dirt, sea turtles have heavy eyelids. This gives them a sleepy look.

Like snakes, turtles do not have ear openings. Instead they have round eardrums just below the skin on the head. These help turtles to feel vibrations (vie-BRAY-shuns) and hear very low sounds. Most turtles are quiet animals and do not vocalize, or make sounds. However, there are some species that do vocalize. Sea turtles may make wailing sounds when they are frightened or hurt. Some tortoise species make loud grunting or moaning sounds when they mate.

Turtles
FUNFACT:

Male common box turtles have red or orange eyes. Females have brown eyes.

Turtles have shells for defense. Turtle shells are tough and give good protection (pro-TEK-shun), but they can be broken. Box turtles have extra protection because they can close their shells up like a box, so that not even a curious dog or fox can bother them. This is because some parts of their shells are hinged. Most turtles cannot close their shells up like boxes and can only pull their legs and head inside for protection.

Shells give some turtles protection from fire. On the grasslands of Africa the grass becomes very dry in the summer. Lightning may cause grass fires that burn very quickly. Some species of turtles are safe inside their shells if the fire burns the dry grass quickly and moves on. If the fire lasts too long, the turtles will die.

Box turtles have hinged shells that close up like a box for protection.

Musk turtles are also called stinkpot turtles because of their strong and unpleasant smell.

Another type of protection is called camouflage (KAM-uh-flaj). Camouflage makes a turtle hard to see. Most turtles move slowly and are not brightly colored. Their shells may simply look like rocks sitting on the ground or partly buried in the ground. Turtles that hibernate have good protection because they usually dig down into the ground in a safe spot and are difficult to see.

Musk is another means of defense. It is a smelly, greasy oil that comes from glands in some animals. Musk turtles have these glands, and they give off a very strong smell. Common musk turtles have such a bad smell they also are known as stinkpot turtles. The strong smell may scare away other animals that might try to hurt the turtle. It also may warn other turtles of danger.

This common map turtle baby is tearing out of its soft, leathery egg.

All baby turtles are hatched from eggs. Some turtle eggs have hard shells, similar to chicken eggs. Some turtle eggs have tough, leathery shells. Some turtles lay only 1 or 2 eggs at a time. Sea turtles are different. Sea turtles may lay over 200 eggs at a time. The larger the female sea turtle, the more eggs she will lay.

Why do sea turtles need to lay so many eggs? Their eggs are buried in the sand at the edge of the ocean. Many things can happen to the eggs and the babies. Many of the babies will not survive and grow. The more eggs there are to begin with, the better the chance that some of them will live to be adults.

Female turtles search for a safe spot away from predators (PRED-uh-torz) to lay their eggs. They also look for a spot where the ground is soft. Most species use their back legs to dig a hole. Once the eggs are laid in the hole, the female covers up the nest and then leaves.

Temperature is important to turtle eggs. For many turtles, the babies will all be males if the temperature of the nest is cool. Females will all be hatched if the temperature of the nest is warm. No one knows why.

Many turtles never live long enough to hatch. Bacteria (bak-TEER-ee-uh) or mold may ruin the eggs. Predators such as coyotes or crocodiles may dig up the eggs. Many baby sea turtles are snatched up and eaten by sea gulls while they are trying to find their way to the ocean.

Turtles
FUNFACT:

Some turtle eggs are round and about the size and shape of a Ping-Pong ball. Others are shaped more like a large bean.

Huge female loggerhead sea turtles drag themselves onto the beach where they dig holes and lay as many as 200 eggs!

The map turtle's name comes from the fine lines on its neck, legs, and shell, which look like roads on a map.

Scientists study turtles of all kinds. They look at turtle shells, skeletons, and even blood vessels. There is still much to be learned about turtles.

Turtles belong to many different families and live in many different ways and places. Some turtles swim in the ocean, some crawl on desert sands, and some burrow underground. Nearly half of all turtles belong to one group or family. This group is called the family of pond and marsh turtles.

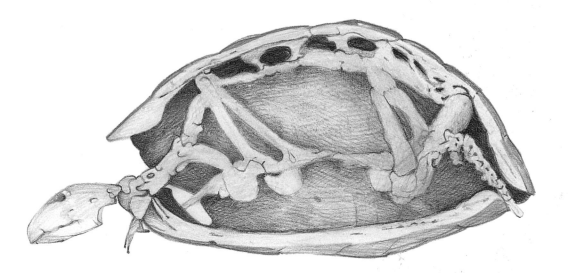

Turtle shells are a part of turtle skeletons and grow from the backbone.

Common box turtles belong to the pond and marsh family and can be found all over the eastern part of the United States. The shells of these turtles may be very dark and unmarked. Other shells may have a lot of yellow or tan spots, lines, and splotches. Their heads may have red or orange or yellow spots, or may be brick red. Box turtles spend most of their time on land, but they will go into water. They can even swim.

During the winter, box turtles hibernate by digging down into the ground. They do not wake up until it is warm again. Box turtles in the cold north may hibernate for 5 or 6 months of the year. In the warm south they may hibernate for only about 2 months of the year. In southern Florida, Texas, and in Mexico they may not hibernate at all.

Turtles
FUNFACT:

In Asia there is a type of box turtle that eats snakes.

Male box turtles have red eyes, but females, like this one, have brown eyes.

Box turtle shells close up like a box. This gives them good protection. It is very hard for a predator to hurt an adult box turtle inside of its shell. However, young box turtles may be eaten if they do not close up their shells quickly enough for protection. They also may be eaten if they are small enough to be swallowed whole or crunched into small pieces. Predators may include badgers, snakes, raccoons, crows, and other animals. Predators also eat box turtle eggs.

Box turtles are sometimes kept as pets. They do well if fed earthworms, dog food, tomatoes, lettuce, fruit, eggs, and bread. They also need water, warmth, and a place to hide.

Another common turtle of the pond and marsh family is the painted turtle. These small 5 to 7 inch (13 to 18 centimeter) turtles are found in many parts of North America. They are found as far north as Canada and as far south as Georgia and Louisiana in the United States.

Painted turtles get their name from their beautiful markings. They have green, red, and yellow lines on their necks and shells. Some of these lines of color are so fine they appear to have been painted on with a tiny paintbrush.

These hardy little turtles can withstand the cold winters of Canada and the much milder winters of the southern United States. In Canada they hibernate through the coldest weather. In the South they are active whenever the sun warms up the waters where they live, even in the middle of winter.

In the wild, painted turtles live in any slow moving body of water, from lakes and ponds to rivers and creeks. They especially like areas where there is soft mud at the bottom and lots of rocks and branches sticking up above the surface of the water. Painted turtles often are found clustered together on these rocks and branches, sunning themselves.

Painted turtles are often kept as pets.

It is easy to see how the painted turtle got its name—
from its beautiful colors and patterns.

The mata mata turtle rests in shallow water where its ridged shell looks more like a rock or a log than a turtle.

Outside of the pond and marsh family are many other, smaller families of turtles.

Mata mata turtles are some of the most unusual turtles in the world. They live in South America in shallow streams and rivers that come off the Amazon River. Mata mata turtle shells are flat with ragged edges. Mata matas also have ragged skin on their heads and necks. They do not move a lot and have a plant called algae (AL-jee) growing on their shells. This gives them good camouflage because it makes them look like a plant-covered rock. Mata matas sit very still on the bottom of a stream. They stretch their long necks so that their long, pointed noses stick out of the water. They use their noses like snorkels to breathe air.

To find food, mata matas move their necks slowly back and forth in the

The Australian snake-necked turtle uses its long neck to reach out and catch fish as they swim by, much like a snake would strike its prey.

water. As fish swim by, mata matas suck water very quickly into their mouths. With the water, they also suck in the fish. Mata matas have very small eyes and poor vision. Scientists think that mata matas do not need good vision because they use their ears to feel the movement of water as fish swim by. This helps them to find and catch their food.

In Australia and South America there are turtles whose necks are so long they are called snake-necked turtles or side-necked turtles. Their necks can be as long as 12 inches (30 centimeters). Their necks are so long they cannot be completely tucked back inside the shell, so they are looped to the side in an "S" curve. These turtles spend almost all of their lives in rivers and only come on land to lay their eggs on the riverbanks. To warm themselves in the sun, they float at the surface of the water. Snake-necked turtles are nocturnal (nok-TURN-ul). That means they are active at night and sleep during the day.

Australian snake-necked turtles reach their long necks up to the water's surface to breathe.

Like mata mata turtles, snake-necked turtles can sit in shallow water and stretch their long necks to the surface for air. They can also move their long necks very quickly for catching fish to eat. In shallow water they may swim along slowly at the surface and stretch their necks down into the water in search of food. This is the way many ducks eat, and it is called dabbling.

Snapping turtles live in fresh water, which is water that is not salty. These turtles snap with their large, powerful jaws. Alligator snapping turtles are the largest of these turtles. The shell of a male can be 30 inches (75 centimeters) long. A male's head can be 10 inches (25 centimeters) across, and a large male can weigh over 200 pounds (90 kilograms).

The tiny red flap of skin on the snapping turtle's tongue acts as a fishing lure.

These large turtles do not move around very much. To catch the fish they eat, they use their special tongues as a lure (LOOR). They lay on the bottom of the river or pond with their mouths open. A worm-shaped piece of their tongue sticks out from the rest of the tongue and wiggles in the water. When hungry fish swim by, they see the wormlike tongue and try to grab it for a quick meal. The alligator snapping turtle snaps its powerful jaws shut and eats the fish. Crayfish, baby alligators, salamanders, snails, crabs, and even other turtles are caught this way. Alligator snapping turtles also eat acorns and fruit that fall into the water.

Snapping turtles may bury their bodies in the mud in shallow water with only their eyes and nostrils peeping above the water so they can see and breathe as they hide.

There are 7 kinds of sea turtles in the world. Sea turtles are turtles that live in the ocean. The green sea turtle lives in the Atlantic Ocean, the Pacific Ocean, and the Indian Ocean. It usually lives in warm water but sometimes it can be found in colder northern waters, too. It has a heart-shaped shell that may be as long as 5 feet (1.5 meters). A large green sea turtle may weigh 400 pounds (180 kilograms), but these larger turtles are becoming more and more rare.

Some people catch and kill green sea turtles for food, or so they can polish the shells to be sold as souvenirs (soo-ven-EARZ) to tourists. In many parts of the world it is illegal to hunt or sell sea turtles since they are an endangered (en-DANE-jurd) species. This means there are not many left in the world. Sadly, in some countries these laws are not enforced or are misunderstood, and the killing of sea turtles continues. In other parts of the world, people do not seem to care that sea turtles are endangered and prize them even more because they are so rare.

Green sea turtles are perfectly adapted to life in the ocean.
Without protection, all sea turtles could become extinct.

x

33

It takes about 20 years for a baby green sea turtle to reach adulthood.

Green sea turtles graze, or look for their food, in large seaweed beds. They eat algae, roots, leaves, and sea grasses. They also eat sponges, snails, jellyfish, and other small ocean animals. They are strong swimmers and may migrate as far as 625 miles (1,000 kilometers) every year between feeding places and nesting grounds.

Like all sea turtles, green sea turtles come onto land to lay their eggs. Females almost always return to the same stretch of beach to lay their eggs each nesting season. They usually nest at night and begin by slowly dragging their large bodies out of the water and up onto the beach. They sniff the sand looking for a nesting site and then dig a hole with their front flippers. About 100 eggs are laid in the nest. The female may return later to dig another nest and lay more eggs. The female may lay as many as 600 eggs in 1 nesting season. Many years later, after female babies have grown, they will somehow find their way back to the same beach where they began life. That is where they will lay their own eggs.

It takes between 50 and 90 days for green sea turtle eggs to hatch. This depends on the temperature of the sand.

The sand must also not become too wet or too dry. The eggs hatch all at once. All the baby turtles must dig together to free themselves from the nest. The babies often hatch after a rainfall and often at night. After they hatch, they must crawl into the ocean on their own.

In the ocean, the green sea turtle babies must find food right away and try to stay safe from predators. It may take as long as 20 years before these babies have grown enough to have babies of their own.

Turtles
FUNFACT:

The inside of a sea turtle's nose swells when it is underwater. This closes off the nose so water does not get in.

Soft-shelled turtles have soft but tough leathery shells and spend all of their lives in shallow fresh water.

Soft-shelled turtles are different from most other turtles. The body of a soft-shelled turtle, including the shell, is covered in a thick, leathery skin. This makes the shell seem softer than the shells of other turtles. The shell is also flatter than the shells of other turtles. Scientists believe these turtles have soft shells because they spend their entire lives in water. There are 22 species of soft-shelled turtles in the world.

Southern or Florida soft-shelled turtles live in lakes, rivers, swamps, marshes, and streams. They spend much of their day buried in the sand or mud at the bottom of the water. While underwater, much of their oxygen (AWK-zih-jin) comes directly from the water. It moves from the water through their leathery skin and into their bodies. In

Like soft-shelled turtles, leatherback sea turtles have soft, tough leathery shells, but they are much larger and live only in salt water.

this way soft-shelled turtles are specially suited to spend much of their lives underwater. They do not need to come to the top to breathe air very often. They also like to float at the surface of the water or bask in the sun on sandbars or riverbanks. Soft-shelled turtles eat mostly snails and insects and some fish. Females may be nearly twice as big as males with a carapace, or upper shell, as long as 24 inches (61 centimeters).

The leatherback sea turtle also has a tough but soft leathery shell. It is not part of the family of soft-shelled turtles, but it looks and lives very much like soft-shelled turtles. One big difference is the type of water these turtles live in. Leatherback turtles live in salt water, in the ocean. Soft-shelled turtles live in fresh water.

Giant tortoises are some of the longest-living animals on earth and may live to be 150 years old.

Tortoises are those turtles that spend most of their lives on land. Most tortoises are found in tropical places where it never freezes. Many tortoises are large, live on islands, and can live for a long time without food. Sailors on long ocean voyages many years ago used to find island colonies of tortoises. They captured the tortoises and carried them onboard their ships for food to last for many months. Sometimes thousands of tortoises were taken from a single island in just 1 year. As a result, some species of tortoises became extinct (ex-TINKD). This means there are no longer any alive. Others became endangered.

Turtles
FUNFACT:

The smallest of all tortoises is the speckled tortoise. It is not quite 4 inches (10 centimeters) when it is fully grown.

The largest of all living tortoises are the Aldabra tortoises. They come from the Aldabra Islands in the Indian Ocean. They are the last of 18 species of tortoises that used to live on islands in the Indian Ocean. Male Aldabra tortoises have a shell that may be as long as 4 feet (122 centimeters). Males weigh as much as 550 pounds (248 kilograms). Females only weigh about 350 pounds (158 kilograms). Scientists believe these tortoises can live to be 150 years old.

Aldabra tortoises live mostly on the grasslands of their islands where they eat all sorts of plants. They even knock over small trees and bushes to get to the leafy parts. This gives the tortoises food and keeps the trees from growing too large. It also allows in more sunlight so that more grass will grow. That way there is always plant food of one kind or another for tortoises to eat.

Turtles
FUNFACT:

The largest turtles in the world are leatherback sea turtles. Large males can weigh 1,300 pounds (585 kilograms). That is more than twice as much as an Aldabra tortoise and about one-tenth the size of an elephant.

Gopher tortoises are important to the survival of many other animals in their habitat.

Gopher tortoises live in the southeastern part of the United States, mostly in Florida. They are unusual tortoises. Like gophers, they burrow underground. They spend much of their lives in the burrows they dig. These burrows are slanted down into the ground at an angle. They may be 10 feet (3 meters) deep and 35 feet (11 meters) long. Gopher tortoises leave their burrows in the middle of the day to find food, and then they return to the burrow.

The burrow makes a home not only for the gopher tortoise, but also for as many as 350 other animals. Most of these are worms, insects, snails, and other tiny creatures. Animals as large as frogs, toads, snakes, opossums, foxes, bobcats, burrowing owls, and bobwhite quail also find safety in the burrows. Without gopher tortoises to make burrows, these other animals would have a much harder time living in their dry, sandy homes. This makes gopher tortoises important to the survival of many other animals.

Terrapins are any kind of water turtle eaten by people. This is especially true of species found in the eastern and southern parts of the United States. Many years ago, terrapin meat was an important meat source for some American Indian tribes and for some settlers and pioneers in rural America. Today turtle meat is rarely eaten by people.

Diamondback (DIE-mond-bak) terrapins live in a large area, from Massachusetts in the northern United States to southern Mexico. They live on the coast, in spots where river water meets ocean water. These places are called estuaries (ESS-chew-air-eez). The water in estuaries is called brackish water, which means it is slightly salty. It is not as salty as seawater, but not as

Turtles
FUNFACT:

Turtles can live a very long time, some for as long as 100 or 150 years. The larger the turtle, the longer it may live.

Diamondback terrapins often cluster together on a log to sun themselves.

fresh as fresh water.

Because they live over such a large area, there are about 7 groups of diamondback terrapins. Each group may look very different from the others. Some may have dark shells, some light shells. Some shells may have orange or yellow edges.

Diamondback terrapins have large, webbed feet for swimming. They spend most of their time in the water, but they usually stay close to the shore. These terrapins, and other turtles, like to climb out of the water and onto land to warm in the sun. Once on land, a whole group may climb on top of each other to try to find a perfect place in the sun. They close their eyes and rest and warm themselves. If one terrapin is frightened, it falls into the water. All of the others quickly follow with a splash.

About 100 years ago these beautiful terrapins were popular as food for people. So many of them were hunted that they nearly became extinct.

As the species has for millions of years, this green sea turtle crawls back into the ocean after coming ashore to lay eggs. Today, it will take help from people for all turtles to survive.

Turtles have been around for many millions of years, moving slowly but surely through the ages. Each species is an important part of its habitat.

Turtles are also important to people. They are an example of ancient reptiles for us to study, and they give us clues about the environment. Turtles do not survive well in places where the water and land are polluted. If turtles are present, it shows that the environment is healthy.

Turtles and their homes need the protection of people. With help, these reptiles will have a chance to live long into the future.

Internet Sites

You can find out more interesting information about turtles and lots of other wildlife by visiting these Internet sites.

www.tortoise.org — California Turtle and Tortoise Club

www.kidsplanet.org — Defenders of Wildlife

http://home.iprimus.com.au/readman/esnt.htm — Eastern Snake-Necked Turtle

www.enchantedlearning.com — Enchanted Learning.com

www.twingroves.district96.k12.il.us/Wetlands/Turtles/PaintedTurtle/PaintedTurtle.html — Kildeer Countryside Virtual Wetlands Preserve

www.discovery.com/exp/turtles/turtles.html — Love and Death on Turtle Beach

www.seaturtlespacecoast.org/learn-about-turtles.html — Sea Turtle Preservation Society

www.scz.org/animals/home.html — Sedgwick County Zoo

www.turtles.org/kids.htm — Turtle Trax Kidz Korner

www.vanaqua.org/Visitor_Information/AquaFacts/Sea_Turtles.htm — Vancouver Aquarium

Index

Aldabra tortoise (*Aldabrachelys gigantea*), 40

Alligator snapping turtle (*Macroclemys temminckii*), 30, 31

Babies, 19, 20, 34, 35

Box turtle (*Terrapene carolina*), 14, 15, 16, 17, 24, 25

Camouflage, 18, 28

Carapace, 8, 37

Chelonian, 7

Chilean tortoise (*Testudo chilensis*), 8

Class Reptilia, 5

Communication, 15

Defense, 16, 18, 25

Desert tortoise (*Gopherus agassizii*), 12, 13

Diamondback terrapin (*Malaclemys terrapin*), 6, 7, 42, 43

Ears, 15, 29

Eggs, 7, 15, 19, 20, 21, 25, 29, 34, 35, 44

Eyes, 15, 25, 29, 31, 43

Food, 10, 11, 12, 14, 15, 24, 28, 29, 30, 31, 34, 35, 37, 39, 40, 41

Giant tortoise (*Geochelone elephantopus*), 10, 38

Gopher tortoise (*Gopherus polyphemus*), 41

Green sea turtle (*Chelonia mydas*), 5, 32, 33, 34, 35, 44

Habitat, 5, 8, 23, 24, 26, 28, 30, 32, 36, 37, 39, 40, 41, 42, 45

Hibernate, 11, 18, 24, 26

Jacobson's organ, 14

Leatherback sea turtle (*Dermochelys coriacea*), 37, 40

Legs, 7, 8, 16, 20, 22

Life span, 38, 40, 42

Loggerhead sea turtle (*Caretta caretta*), 21

Map turtle (*Graptemys geographica*), 8, 10, 19, 22

Mata mata (*Chelus fimbriatus*), 28, 30

Mating, 14, 15

Musk turtle (*Sternotherus odoratus*), 18

Neck, 22, 26, 28, 29, 30

Nest, 20, 34, 35

Painted turtle (*Chrysemys picta*), 26, 27

Pets, 25, 26

Plastron, 8

Predator, 20, 25, 35

Sea turtle (*Cheloniidae*), 5, 12, 15, 19, 20, 21, 32, 33, 34, 35, 44

Shell, 5, 7, 8, 9, 10, 11, 16, 17, 18, 19, 22, 23, 24, 25, 26, 28, 29, 30, 32, 36, 37, 40, 43

Side-necked turtle (*Phrynops geoffroanus*), 29

Skutes, 8

Snake-necked turtle (*Chelodina siebenrocki*), 29, 30

Snapping turtle (*Chelydra serpentina*), 30, 31

Soft-shelled turtle (*Pelodiscus sinensis*), 8, 36, 37

Speckled tortoise (*Homopus signatus*), 40

Spiny turtle (*Heosemys spinosa*), 8

Texas tortoise (*Gopherus berlandieri*), 9

Tongue, 31

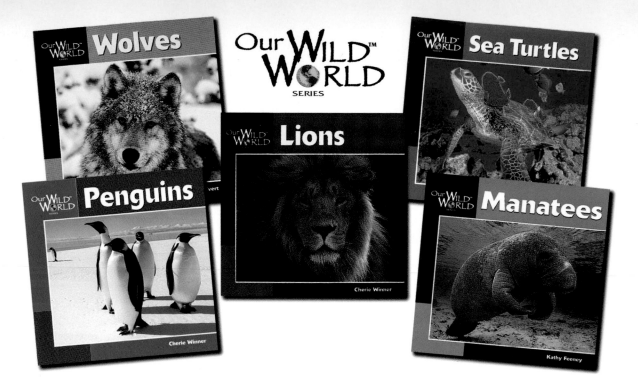

Titles available in the Our Wild World Series:

ALLIGATORS AND CROCODILES
ISBN 1-55971-859-9

BISON
ISBN 1-55971-775-0

BLACK BEARS
ISBN 1-55971-742-4

CARIBOU
ISBN 1-55971-812-9

CHIMPANZEES
ISBN 1-55971-845-5

COUGARS
ISBN 1-55971-788-2

DOLPHINS
ISBN 1-55971-776-9

EAGLES
ISBN 1-55971-777-7

GORILLAS
ISBN 1-55971-843-9

LEOPARDS
ISBN 1-55971-796-3

LIONS
ISBN 1-55971-787-4

LIZARDS
ISBN 1-55971-857-9

MANATEES
ISBN 1-55971-778-5

MONKEYS
ISBN 1-55971-849-8

MOOSE
ISBN 1-55971-744-0

ORANGUTANS
ISBN 1-55971-847-1

PENGUINS
ISBN 1-55971-810-2

POLAR BEARS
ISBN 1-55971-828-5

SEA TURTLES
ISBN 1-55971-746-7

SEALS
ISBN 1-55971-826-9

SHARKS
ISBN 1-55971-779-3

SNAKES
ISBN 1-55971-855-2

TIGERS
ISBN 1-55971-797-1

TURTLES
ISBN 1-55971-861-7

WHALES
ISBN 1-55971-780-7

WHITETAIL DEER
ISBN 1-55971-743-2

WOLVES
ISBN 1-55971-748-3

See your nearest bookseller, or order by phone 1-800-328-3895

NorthWord Press
Chanhassen, Minnesota